Jesus Is…God, Son, or Both

By a Witness, May Lewis

Editor: La'Brenda Hill

Citations: Nelson, Thomas. (2007). Holy Bible (King James Version). Nashville, TN.

"All scriptures are from the book and version stated above unless otherwise indicated."

First Printing: 2020
ISBN: 978-1-71649-949-4
MAY LEWIS
Lincoln, NE 68512
USA

Dedication

This book is dedicated, first, to the Almighty God. It was written to give God the glory and the praise while in the process of feeding His sheep. I also want to give, what I call a "shout out", to God and thank Him especially for giving me the life that I have. Even if I would have been able to do things differently, my life still would not have been a better outcome than it is right now. Readers, do not get me wrong, it has not all been ice cream with a cherry on the top. I have had some sorrows too, but there could have been a whole lot more pain. I am so glad that my great times have prevailed all of the sorrows.

My next dedication goes out to the Books of the Bible, in which I mediate on frequently. Of course, while reading, I might have lost some sleep on some days and nights. The important part is that I gained a better insight on life and God.

In addition, I have to give a special dedication to the entire world. Maybe one day we will all be knitted together as one big family in unity. We will then be able to get along with each other peaceably and love each other unconditionally as God has loved us.

TABLE OF CONTENTS

FOREWORD

My mom and grandma often stated, "One of the best things in the world is to get a good understanding." This is why this particular book is so important so that it will give you a true insight of what's being talked about at school, on the job, at home, on television, and in the church. Under their same breath, in the same conversations, certain beliefs are frequently stated this way, and then the next thing you hear it is stated in another way. Which way is it? Is Jesus actually God? Or, is Jesus actually the Son of God? Or, is Jesus both God and the Son? Yes, these are the lingering questions. So which one is it, this, or that, or is it this and that?

Can you imagine how confusing those statements sound? Especially to someone that does not believe. Better yet, even to those individuals who are scared to ask for clarification of the matter it can be confusing. On the other hand, it could even be more confusing to those who have grown up in the church and now hear something very different from what he or she has been custom to hearing. This is why it is best to read the Bible for yourself. We have to get into a closer relationship with God and with His Word for guidance to reveal the truth to us in the Spirit. *"Know ye that the Lord he is God: it is he that hath made us, and not we ourselves; we are his people, and the sheep of his pasture" (Psalm 100:3 King James Version).* The fact remains that God is still God, the Creator that made us. This has not changed.

Back in my head, I can still remember the question that was asked by an instructor whether Jesus is God. He asked, "Did anyone want to comment on the matter?" Although, I knew what the answer should be, the particular feeling that I had at that time did not really want to do a one-on-one debate with the instructor. I knew where this might lead. I did not speak on the topic. However, I still felt deep down inside that I should have said something. At that moment, I knew how Peter must have felt when he had heard the rooster crow. This book was established to give everyone an avenue to answering that type of question and backing it up with some Biblical scriptures.

I can see clearer why wisdom is better than any amount of money. I realize now that back then it was not my time to elaborate on the subject. I believe that God was waiting for a time and platform like this one. A platform where I could explain and where many others, not just the ones in the classroom, would be getting a good understanding to whether Jesus is God, the Son, or Both.

Chapter 1

THE ORIGINATOR

Can you imagine for a moment what we would have said today if Jesus had done those same miracles as He did in the Biblical days in front of us? Of course, you know we would have had an excuse for all of them. For example, when Jesus turned water into wine. We would have said things like, "His daddy must have taught Him how to make moonshine," or "that particular trait came from His mother's side of the family because she was a great cook." Another example was when Jesus had made a blind man see. We would have said, "He used something He had gotten from the drug store," or "the red dirt used had many vitamins in it". Then another example was when Jesus raised the man from the dead. We would have said, "A jackleg doctor pronounced him dead," or "the man must have been stoned drunk." We would have made excuses after excuses. Could it be that Jesus had done all of these miracles just because He may have been God, the Originator who made Heaven and earth and the One who was there from the beginning?

The word "lord" is often mentioned and reference in the Bible for persons in leadership or persons whom you have the deepest respect. The word "Lord" also referred to God and the Son of God (with a capital L). Others who were referred to as lords in Bible were: husbands, kings, angels, masters, gods, etc. Various individuals often called Jesus by different names, such as, Master, Lord, Teacher, Savior, God, etc. With Jesus being able to perform numerous of signs, wonders, and miracles, they wondered, and were sort of puzzled on what particular title should be given to a man who could do many incredible things. They knew that one of the notable names for Jesus was to call Him Lord, and they often referred to Him with that name from time to time.

David had also emphasized that the Lord had said to his Lord. David indicates that there were two individuals referred to as Lord with a capital "L." Does not this show that both Jesus and God were called Lord in the Bible? Jesus was to sit on the right of God until God makes Jesus' enemies His footstool. Even though the word "Lord" has oftentimes been referred to both Jesus and God, Jesus emphasized that there is only but one Father. *"And call no man your father upon the earth: for one is your Father, which is in heaven" (Matthew 23:9).* We should not be calling anyone else our Father. There are other names we can use to call our earthly dads, such as: daddy, papa, pops, etc. It makes you wonder why do some think that there can be so many gods out there, but only one dad. Let's remember what Jesus had implied earlier, that you can have only one Father, does not this also mean only one God?

A number of individuals and things have been described as a so-called god. How many really were the actual God? That is the God with a capital "G." We know that there should be only one G-O-D. Part of one of the Ten Commandments stated that we should not bow down nor to serve and worship any other gods and that the Lord was a jealous God.

Jesus has many attributes that constitute Him as being God. How about Jesus knowing all about how it was in Heaven and often mentioning the difference between Heaven and earth. People have wondered how Jesus could talk about what Heaven is actually like unless He's been there. Could Jesus be God in the flesh since God had the power to have walked around in Heaven, then came down to earth and talked about it?

We cannot forget the healing power Jesus had. Jesus had healed a person that was sick with palsy. Jesus emphasized to him that his sins were forgiven. The scribes disputed that only God could forgive sins. *"Why doth this man thus speak blasphemies? who can forgive sins but God only" (Mark 2:7)?* That statement helps signify that Jesus must have been, in some way, be God in order to forgive sins. Do not forget about Jesus raising individuals from the dead. Did not some of the disciples raise some people from the dead too? So what does this make them?

Jesus showed many times that He could do incredible things. Whether Jesus is God is still the pondering question. The best thing is to know God for yourself. You have to get into a good relationship with God. Yes, you have to ask God for guidance and meditate on His Words in the Bible day and night; day in and day out. You will be surprised after reading the Bible many times of some of the things that you might have failed to see. This is what makes this book so wonderful. Just keep on reading! This book will assist you in getting the best understanding in order to get the answer to that pondering question of whether Jesus is God.

Chapter 2

THE WAGERS ARE HIGHER

Today, there are so many different types of positions in the church available for you to maintain. Even though some of their names may not be as familiar as the pastor's is, such as: the Missions' Specialist, Christian Educator, Food Service Director, Director of Counseling, etc. Nevertheless, the common denominator factor among these positions has not changed. The accountability for those positions still has higher wagers. It is much higher than any other job position that you will ever hold in the world.

Most individuals take on these occupations in church just to receive a break in their taxation and to get higher wages, but it is more to it than attaining a tax break or a salary. They forget what is really at stake when you are one of the officials of God's House. When I mentioned wagers do not get confused with this word "wagers" verses the word "wages." These professions should not be taken lightly. God does not want His sheep to be lead astray in any kind of way. The pastors are not the only one that is on the so-called podium. These positions are held more accountable and are at a higher standard as well as they should be held by people who walk in the ways of God. *"For a bishop must be blameless, as the steward of God; not self-willed, not soon angry, not given to wine, no striker, not given to filthy lucre" (Titus 1:7);* Each church position held should be equipped with a person being trustworthy, ethical, filled with the Holy Spirit, and knowledgeable of God's Word. They should all be about doing God's business just as Jesus was. In addition, their spouses and children who live in their household should be a reflection of them.

When you hold a position in the church, it should be as important as anything that may be life threatening to you. Because your life certainly depends on what you do and how great you portray yourself while you are in those positions. We should take notes from Jesus and become as furious as He was when someone tried to treat the church as being about a man's business instead of being about God's business.

Not only should the jobs in God's House not be taken lightly, but even the anointing oil should not be taken lightly. The anointing oil should be available for pastors only to administer to other pastors (or God's chosen). The oil is holy and is not for anyone else to dispense and use except for what it was intended. *"Upon man's flesh shall it not be poured, neither shall ye make any other like it, after the composition of it: it is holy, and it shall be holy unto you" (Exodus 30:32).* Neither should anyone be trying to duplicate anything like the oil. Just like the Ark of the Covenant could not be touched by everyone, the oil should be viewed just as sacred.

We have to get in the mindset of trying to please God and less of a mindset concentrating on pleasing individuals. Have you ever heard of any church officials or any organization leaders in this day and time stating that "enough was enough," and for you to stop giving? Or, does their wealth just overflow, similar to the rich man that had more than enough food and wanted to build a bigger barn instead of giving some to the needy. How about churches being similar now as they purchase more and more properties, such as, buildings, planes, etc., rather than help the needy out of the abundance of their funds? Remember, we should never be so greedy and selfish or so captivated on what we have that we cannot share and help God's people in hardship. The church should be all about God's business. It is not about investing the church's money into buying other buildings, planes, etc., especially when the investment is more of a liability rather than an investment in the church and God's people. It should not take money

18

away from the church. It should be all about bettering the church rather than bringing it into bankruptcy. It's all about taking care of God's house first, then taking care of God's people, and not taking care of the businesses by using the tithes and the offering funds unwisely and/or sinfully.

In addition, during the process of beautifying the churches, we should not get so fascinated in putting up decorations that we leave out the décor pertaining to God's Commandments, His Agreements, and the Bible. All of these should be placed in plain sight in the church for all to see. I do have to give credit that some churches do display the names of the tribes of Israel, but still, when you look around, God's Commandments, Agreements, and the Bible are nowhere to be seen or as visible.

One question that I hear a lot is: "What's the reason behind why there are so few men in church"? My statement to my readers is: "God always will give you what you need at the right time." If there are more women than men in the congregation, then use them. In the Biblical days, women were part of some crucial events in history. Deborah was an important leader that prophesized and judged Israel. Ruth was loyal by helping and sticking with her mother-in-law, and both were widows. Jael had guts and hammered a nail in the head of the evil Captain Sisera. Queen Esther was unselfish and helped save her nationality from being destroyed. Women can be very significant in different positions in the church, just try them. If Jesus could have used stones to praise and glorify God, why can we not use women? If God is no respecter of persons, so why are we?

We have to remember the true job in the church is to be all about God and Jesus. It is not to be all about self or trying to make the most money. The positions that you hold in church have major impact on the individuals' souls as well as your own. This is why there is more answerability when you hold these positions in church. An important thing to remember is that we should all at least go out of our way, in some kind of form or fashion, and teach someone about God and Jesus every day. It should not matter what position you hold in the church or even out of church. God uses us all whether a man or woman. We need to take a page from the disciples who taught about God and Jesus every day in church as well as at people's houses. Yes, God should be put first, and He should be the centerpiece of our jobs and our lives.

Chapter 3

THE OFFSPRING

Without a doubt, we can say that we are all made in the image of God. We are God's children, His sons and daughters. Shouldn't Jesus also be called His Son since He was made in God's image too, and not being God Himself? It is sort of strange when you think about it. Most of us can agree that Jesus was a descendant of David in his family tree line. Yet some of us somehow get kind of baffled when it comes to whether Jesus is God Himself in the flesh, or whether Jesus is just the offspring, or whether Jesus is both God and the Son.

Certain things come back to memory when I recall some of the Bible Studies with the boys. It makes me recognize the true meaning of how iron sharpens iron. Each one of them had a reflection of how the Word was revealed to them. You are able to get another person's perspective on the understanding of the Bible just like how the Bible was written with different individuals' accounts of the Gospel. You will be surprised at what person can give you a revelation of the Word, or whom God will be speaking through to get a Word to you, regardless of status or age. God asked us to not only read His Word, but also be constantly doers of His Word. Jesus was a true advocate of the Word. He did not stop giving the Gospel to all He had encountered. Jesus often emphasized that He was doing the Will of God and not His own desires. Could this also be why Jesus always had great knowledge of God's Word, because He was God's Son and iron sharpens iron too?

A voice was heard when Jesus had gotten baptized. *"And lo a voice from heaven, saying, This is my beloved Son, in whom I am well pleased" (Matthew 3:17).* Was not this God letting us know that Jesus was His Son? In addition, was not this God telling us how much He adores His Son?

God has giving everyone the option to do right or to keep doing wrong in this world. Jesus was a prime example of what doing right was all about. Yet, Jesus did not want to be recognized as being "good." *"And Jesus said unto him, Why callest thou me good? there is none good but one, that is God" (Mark 10:18).* Jesus let the wealthy man know immediately that He was not to be called "good." The Father God Almighty is the only one that is good and no one else. Was not this also an implication from Jesus, letting us know that He was not God? How about this question, is it not implying that Jesus was an offspring of God when the devil tempted Jesus? The devil acknowledged if Jesus was the Son of God He should be able to do many different things; but Jesus did not bite into what the devil was saying, and kept disputing him with the Word. Better yet, was it not also revealed that Jesus was not God when Peter stated that God raised Jesus His Son from the dead?

Many people may have missed what Jesus was emphasizing and meaning which was that someone else sent Him to come down to this earth instead of Him sending Himself. Was Jesus letting us know that He was not alone and that there was a higher being over Him? Could this higher being who Jesus spoke about not only be His Father but God too?

Jesus came into this world to save us, He gave his flesh and blood so that we may live and have eternal life. He did not come into this world to condemn us. He came to save us. It makes you wonder why we still do not know who He really is? That is, whether Jesus is God, the Son, or whether He is Both?

Chapter 4

LOVE ALL

L-O-V-E is a powerful thing. Love is more potent than faith and hope. *"And now abideth faith, hope, charity, these three; but the greatest of these is charity" (1 Corinthians 13:13).* Some may say or even think that faith and hope are above love, but I like to say, "What does the Bible say" but for my readers, "What is in the Bible?"

Since love is so imperative, we are supposed to love all. Now tell me why is "love" not the number one talked about topic? The pastors should be harping on this sermon in churches. Why are not the teachers also lecturing about it in schools? Even the parents should make sure that love is being displayed every day in their homes. Love should be a hot talked about topic for the kids instead of reality and political television shows.

Are you still wondering why there is so much killing, hating, backstabbing, and disrespecting, etc.?

Where is the L-O-V-E? Love is the one remedy that is missing in our lives. Love is so nonexistent these days. That is why we are the only one of God's creatures who go out to kill just for the fun of it, and not for any vital reasons, such as: to eat, or for protecting our love ones or ourselves from danger. Jesus knew just how important love was that He summed it all up in two Commandments for us to follow. The first one was to love God with all your heart, soul, and mind, and this coincides with the first four of the Ten Commandments. The second one was to love your neighbor, which correspond with the last six of the Ten Commandments. Both of Jesus' Commandments should be put before our own selfish needs because this is what love is all about.

The true meaning of love was best exhibited by God. He demonstrated how powerful love really is. He gave up His Son out of the love He had for us, the sinners. Jesus was sent to eliminate the desire to sin, keeping us from devilish behavior and teaching us how to love one another. To show how far we are from the true meaning of love we find it difficult to even unite in the Churches. Churchgoers cannot display to the non-goers on how to be as one. Pastors are unable to unite together in one building; but have to build a church beside, across, down, or on the other corner away from each other. These buildings are not being built as if the churches were overflowing with people. You may see less than a hand full of folks in each church. We should not be building churches in close proximity to each other. We should be building churches in areas that do not have a church in their vicinity to familiarize those individuals that have little or no knowledge of God and Jesus. There is too much dissension among us and not enough love. How can we say we love God when we won't come together to fellowship in the same church? It is even difficult for us to help out our neighbors when we see and know they are in need. In addition, we do not have compassion for them. It should not matter whether a person is a church member or not.

We sometimes ask God for a million dollars to furnish and do the devil's work and then we wonder why we have not received it. Can you not comprehend why God will not give you a million dollars to fund cars (not just one), houses (to be bigger than a neighbor's), lusting after many women and men (to sleep around with), and an excessive amount of clothes and jewelries, etc.? We probably had not one time asked God to let us be a millionaire to help others, or not to only start a business, but also to use the business to help the poor and unemployed individuals to have jobs. This also reminds me of Demetrius, the silversmith, who was more concerned about making more money and not allowing anything to interfere with his assets. He should have been more concern about believing there is only one God. We should be asking to be more of a giving person than becoming more of a recipient. I guess you can see why we will still be waiting for a million dollars. Better yet, why don't we ask God to teach us how to love and do righteousness, not asking for money, lascivious things, or over indulging in food, etc.? Instead, teach us how to put God first before all others and anything, and then we will begin to see how things begin to fall into place.

It does not cost us one cent to love. However, it is worth more than all the money and gold in the world. You can say that it is definitely priceless. Yep, it costs no amount of money as stated, but it does come with a price. If you do not have it, you could lose your soul. You would be worthless. If God is really your Father, you should be all about what is right, and not what the devil wants, which is for you to be about doing what is evil and wrong.

I have always admired how David was able to write so many, many prayers and poems to God. I was meditating on God's Word one midnight and decided that I wanted to give writing a poem a try and as long as it came from deep down inside my heart, I knew that I should be okay. Once I started writing, the words kept flowing and it was like I could not stop. It continued as I was heading towards the bathroom. Of course, I start thinking that I needed to get some rest. That's funny I had wanted more than just a few lines and now I was getting it, and then I found an excuse to want to stop. So typical...hum! The poem below is about true love, and guess what...that is the title (Ha..Ha!).

True Love

You are always there through the darkest time as well as the lightest, which in both you make my smile still shine bright.
I can always count on you.
I don't mind getting on my knees for you not to beg, but to show honor and gratitude.
You have been there before day one, and continue after days here on this earth.
You love me to the fullest, which made me replicate that love to you.
The love you cannot get on a street corner, an office block, or neither in a mailbox.
The kind that keeps you warm day and night thru storms and winter.

This true love that makes you want to tell everyone whether they listen or not.
The kind that you want everyone to experience not the fly by night kind.
The kind that makes you want to study, read, and do your Words of what you want.
One day I will see that smile that often shine bright in me.
I can tell you how your true love always carries me.
The way you are the first thing on my mind when I wake up in the morning and the last thing on my mind when I go to bed.
How learning about Jesus taught me how to be all about what you want of me and not my selfish desires.
I will always give you my heart and trust in you.
I know you will never break my heart.
Help me and guide me so I will never break yours.

On this last note regarding love, I would like to leave you with this: It does not matter if you have done everything in this world, given all the money in the world to others, been to all the different places in this world, or even owned everything in the world, if you have not loved, it doesn't mean a thing. *"And though I have the gift of prophecy, and understand all mysteries, and all knowledge; and though I have all faith, so that I could remove mountains, and have not charity, I am nothing" (1 Corinthians 13:2).* This verse shows you loud and clear how powerful love is. We have to convey love. God is love. His love is never-ending.

Chapter 5

THE ODDS

Hopefully, the previous chapters have gotten you thinking a little bit. Jesus has done some incredible things. By being able to do those things, what are the odds that Jesus could actually be both, God and the Son? Jesus had often emphasized that the Father and Him were alike. Did God actually come down and transform Himself into Jesus? It may make you wonder how someone could have done the things that Jesus had done if He was not God Himself.

Jesus and God were on one accord with the same goal. Which may cause some people to wonder how could they have possibly been a separate entity? Even the Jews wanted to kill Jesus because they believed Jesus was placing Himself on the same plateau as God. Jesus made it known to us from the beginning that God and Jesus are in unity as one. *"Believe me that I am in the Father, and the Father in me: or else believe me for the very works' sake"*

(John 14:11). Jesus let us know that when you look at Him you should see God because their ways are the same. It is hard to consider or think about all the miracles and signs that Jesus had done, and it would not have been possible if God were not part of Him. The only way to get through the Father was to go through Jesus. Is Jesus both entities? Could Jesus actually be God, to know exactly what God always wanted to do? That's why He was able to follow God's Words to the letter.

When Jesus was talking to the Samaritan woman at the well, was He actually implying that He could have been both God and the Son? *"Jesus answered and said unto her, If thou knewest the gift of God, and who it is that saith to thee, Give me to drink; thou wouldest have asked of him, and he would have given thee living water" (John 4:10).* Was Jesus letting her know that He was God, and He had the power to do and to supply all things? In addition, was He letting her know that He was God and knew about all things, and she could not hide anything from Him? Is that also why He could tell her about herself and her husbands?

Paul routinely talked about Jesus in the Jewish synagogues and in the market places. Epicureans and Stoicks philosophers even believed Jesus was a strange god that Paul had kept mentioning. They contested repeatedly what Paul was saying about Jesus believing only God could have really done those things that Jesus had done.

God is a Spirit, the Holy Spirit, in which He can be anything or anyone that He wants to be at any given time and He can be everywhere. We need to remember that God dwells in us, which is the Holy Ghost. The Holy Ghost teaches us all about the way we should live. Could it be that we are just watching too much television, and it has too much influence on the way we act and think? We're thinking that God turned into Jesus like an animation character, and then came down from Heaven to the earth then went back to Heaven and turned back into being God.

Otherwise, could we be actually thinking that it is too good to be true; that someone would love us so much to let their Son die for something that He did not do, to be a Savior for us all? Can it be that we mainly feel this way because we would not have done such a thing ourselves? What it all boils down to is that perhaps we are thinking this way because Jesus had too much power for one man, so He must be both, God and the Son.

Chapter 6

FINDING YOUR FORTE AND CALLING

This chapter hit close to home for me. I had deep feelings towards it and almost thought about writing a book on it. Your plans may not be God's plans for you even if they are your forte. Did you stop first to check in with God to see what His plan was for you? Rest a sure those talents that you learned from doing your own agenda will still play a vital role in what God's plan is for you. If not, believe me, it would not have taken place. God has more in this life for you to do according to His purpose, and it's your calling, not your dream. Just because you are good in it does not mean it is your calling.

Can I go ahead and tell you a little about my forte? Or, should I have said my dream? I will try to be brief (Try...LOL!!). This particular skill was my best side or my strong side. Yes, I was truly talented in it.

__My Forte:__ This particular talent that I acquired was based on getting tired of listening to girls talk about, "she *say,"..."he say." One day, I picked up a ball to get away from all the noise making. This ball became my skill. My skill not to brag was good enough for a group of guys to be talking about in the same conversation when each side had a heated debate going back and forth about the same person (on who was the best girl basketball player), and each side did not know it until later on in the conversation. Later on, one of the guys stated that he shouldn't be telling me about that conversation. He stated that it might swell up my head. Can you just imagine...this incident had happened after my prime. I use to shoot the "cover off" the basketball. You could count the ones I missed on one hand, if any. Many times I was asked, "did you miss"? There were all kinds of names for me, such as automatic, eagle's eye, etc. I always said when my shot was blocked, "You have to block them all." If not, the one that you did not block will fall, and will be the game winning shot (and they were).*

Not only was I a great shooter, but I also had a great instinct for the game. Although I was a medium height for a girl, I was able to out rebound some of the guys. I could out test where the ball would come off after a shot and I was already up there and getting the ball before the guys started jumping, and many were great high leapers. Of course, my ball handling was not bad either, and some guys though they just could take it (of course, you reach...) and the ball players knew the rest of the story. Do not let me talk about my defense. I could go on, but I said I would be brief (Try…LOL!!).

I can truly say that I played against and with some professional players, both men and women, especially men. Both basketball and football players that I played against were at the top of their game. I was considered a legend and that is no joke. I had really thought my calling was to be the "World's Best Lady Basketball Player." I used to eat and sleep basketball. I was not doing what I should have done, and that was to put God first. Yet, I was faithful, and you can say faithful to the ball.

Do not let your talent, job, person, etc. dictate who you are. I have heard this following statement many times: "When you play a sport the majority of your life, it is hard to find and do something else." If that's the case then you have let that sport dictate your life instead of God. It's the same with people and their bank accounts when it has been depleted, and the same goes when your house or car has been taken away or you have to sale it for whatever reason. It also goes for individuals when you let a person dictate your life instead of God. As long as you are breathing, your life goes on. You're able to rebound and bounce back and do anything within God's plan, just put God first. Don't forget, God gave Job way more than what he had at first. God gave you life, so use it. Now go out, be productive with your life.

God gave Bezaleel, in the spirit, different abilities to work on the tabernacle. God has given all of us talents. In these talents we all have different abilities too. If one is lacking in a particular skill, the other individual has the necessary ability to assist them and then they can work together in unity. This is what makes us so successful. God constantly gives us what we need, and it is always at the right time.

Do you hear something…is that your calling that's calling you? Are you going to answer? If it's your calling that you hear and you do it, you will always succeed (whether it's spiritually, physically, or financially) in it. Just make sure whatever you do, you do it in the name of the Lord, and do it morally. Do it with all your might so that you will be pleasing to God and not to human beings. *"But as he which hath called you is holy, so be ye holy in all manner of conversation; Because it is written, BE YE HOLY; FOR I AM HOLY" (1Peter 1:15-16).* Make sure that you do not do it in any way to dishonor God, but giving God all the glory and praise.

__My Calling:__ I guess you can say this one is more transparent for you to see. Guess what... right now you are reading it! This one I did not see coming, not even a mile away. I had no intent of writing. This was nowhere on my agenda. It was not in my game plan. It is something I enjoy doing, and it's very relaxing. I'm riding the waves on this one while bringing more people closer to our Father God.

I remember one of my instructors asked me was I going to write a book. I said quickly, no! Not knowing that God was getting me equipped in college whose mission was all about Jesus, to pursue what God had planned for me. God was paving the way for me to be stronger in His Word. I was disgusted by all the papers I had to write for homework assignments. I just did not know God's plan.

When I looked back, I believe God has been working on this one for some time now. I remembered when I was younger, my English teachers always asked each year to write about what you did during the summer. I was always empty for words to write (funny how things change). However in junior high (middle) school, I was great in English Grammar Class. I was asked by my teacher to assist her in grading papers, and I received a Certificate of Achievement. Somehow when I got in high school, I guess you could say that my love for English dropped (or, I got grown. LOL!), or you can say different teaching styles also helped. I do believe this is what God wanted me to do for some time now, and I am glad to be of service.

Just as Esther being the queen, it was not her calling, but her dream. Her actual calling was to free her nationality from being persecuted. She was brought in the right place at the right time to do this. Her uncle let her know that if she didn't do it then help would come from someone else, but by then her kinfolks would already be demolished.

Basketball was not my calling either, but it did have its purpose. The attributes that I learned while playing made me a better person. It taught me about leadership, being a team player, how to be fearless, loyalty, competitiveness, commitment, hard worker, love for others, and respect for each other. It was not just all about playing basketball. It was about life. Now I understand the full picture. As my mom used to say: "You will understand it better by and by." The love for basketball made me a true warrior. You can say that I am now a true warrior for God with the same commitment. It has been a wonderful journey. Thanks to God, I did not lose focus. He was developing my characteristics as a working sheep for Him. So when I think about all the life lessons I have learned, I am so grateful. I can enjoy God as I enjoyed basketball, but let me tell you that enjoying God is much better.

I thanked God as well as asked God to forgive me for not pursuing and taking advantage of some of the talents that He had given me the way that I should have. In addition, I want to thank God for blessing me with more than one talent; and I asked God to help me use any of those talents to draw more souls to Him. I am aiming for what I call and created a new name that is a "zilliouls." What "zilliouls" means is feeding a zillion souls about God through the gospel of Jesus Christ (the Good News). That is my goal as well as my calling, to feed God's sheep through my books.

We cannot do anything without God. But we can do all things as long as we do what God wants for us in His plan. God wants us to get into a closer relationship with Him by reading the Bible, meditating on His Word, and doing what He asks of us. We have to listen to what God puts on our hearts and allow God to lead us into whatever we decide to do, and then we will be justified in doing it. By putting God first in everything that we do, we will see the success in whatever we put our hands on. Make sure we give thanks to God whether we are able to do our forte or not. Do not stop giving God the praises that are due Him. Do not stop praying for everyone and everything. Whatever situation you are in be joyful and grateful. *"To every thing there is a season, and a time to every purpose under the heaven" (Ecclesiastes 3:1):* God has stamped a date and time for everything we do.

We have to remember just because we are good at our talent does not mean it is what God has called us to do. I want to encourage you to still follow your dream. Your calling may not be your dream, but it may lead you in the right direction, and give you the ability to overachieve in your forte. These skills will help you later on in your calling. God has a plan for you. He has giving us all talents, but not all the same talents. What we do with these gifts is up to us. Do not put it to rest or waste it! **Resting and wasting our talents is the reason why it so much hidden talent in this world that has not come to the surface yet.** God would bless us with even more talents if we make use of the gift that He has already given us. God has the final say-so of what our true vocation may be. We need to enjoy every minute and take advantage of the talents that God has given us. We need to enjoy the ride and do the best that we can do in whatever field we occupy.

Even though everything pointed toward Moses for taking the Israelites to the Promised Land, he also did the legwork for taking the Israelites out of Egypt. It was not Moses' calling. Moses did not know at first, but he was also getting Joshua ready. Be mindful of what you are doing and who may be round you watching what you are doing. Always try to do your best because you may be preparing someone else to do what you thought was your calling. Sometimes it may take two to three generations of preparations before it comes to pass. God may have another plan. You may prepare someone, then that person may prepare someone else. It may not have been for you, nor your children, but it may have been your grandkids' calling.

We must remember that everyone is here on this earth for a brief period. We need to take advantage of the moments that we have by loving and serving one another with those talents God gave us. Reach for your goal as high as you can. If it is not God's calling for you, He will lead you toward the real destiny He has for you. You will want to do it for the rest of your life. It will give you peace and joy when you do it. God will give us a vocation that will not cause us to say how talented we are or how good we are, but how great God is!

Chapter 7

PRAY LIMITLESS

I have learned more and more about the importance of praying. Especially when it comes to safeguarding the ones you love when you are not able to be with them every day and everywhere. When you care deeply about someone, you want to protect them in any way you can. You want to keep them from any harm and danger. Who is better at doing that than God Almighty Himself? He is a better protector, more powerful, and can be everywhere at the same time. I knew that I had to be in a better prayer life with God; and not only for my love ones sakes, but also for mine. Especially with everything that is happening today in this world, I knew that I had to keep praying to God; praying, praying, and praying without any boundaries.

There is no reason why we should ever want to stop praying. We should always ask God for the ability to have the desire to want to pray. As I mentioned previously in my book, "<u>You Want to Stop Sinning…Stop,</u>" there is always someone or something (yes, that means everybody and everything) that you can always pray for, no matter who you are. You will never run out of what to talk about. Nor do you have to know who they are before you pray for them. It also does not matter who is right or wrong, who did it or did not do it, or the reason behind why it was done. We need to pray and ask for forgiveness for all. We have to have that unconditional love for others that God has for us. Praying is not all about ourselves (being selfish) nor is it always about our immediately family. We are not in this world alone and you never know when you pray who maybe around the corner and you kept that person from doing you bodily harm.

Praying is about talking to God continuously and having a good rapport. Why not tell God about your day. Just as we keep in tune with our friends (He's better than a friend) by holding a conversation with them about what's going on in our lives, the same should be for God. Why not keep Him in tune. We need to have an open communication to God. We have to keep the line of communication open. We should always tell God how much we appreciate and love Him. We need to also tell Him how much we want to do what He wants us to do, and follow within His plan for us, by doing His Will. Your prayers can be short or long. If your knees hurt from you being on them too long, the more you do pray on them, the less it hurts. God takes the pain away. Your prayers do not always have to be on your knees. If there are medical reasons and you are not able to bend down on your knees, God knows your ability and your heart. At times, I have had a quick chat with God right before speaking to an audience or individual asking God for guidance. The person sitting or standing right there in front of me never knew I was praying. Yes, I was referring to God to make a decision.

You are not worrying God when you pray. God wants us to come to Him. If we are struggling a little bit when trying to communicate to God, we can ask Jesus for help. Even the disciples wanted to ensure they gave God all the praise so they asked Jesus how to pray to God. I always have loved the pattern of the Lord's Prayer that Jesus gave the disciples. This example helped them to learn how to pray to the Father.

The Bible referenced the Lord's Prayer in several sections. The verses that I will be relating to are located in the Book of Matthew. One night I was meditating on the Word and was falling half-asleep while reading Matthew 6:9-13. I believe that for me this is when I am most submissive in listening. The following paragraph is what came to my mind that night. My thoughts are in parenthesis after each verse.

I will go over what was revealed to me for verses "9-13." I will first start off with verse number nine. *"After this manner therefore pray ye: Our Father which art in heaven. Hallowed be thy name"* (God, honor His holy name*)*.

The next one is verse number ten. *"Thy kingdom come. Thy will be done in earth, as it is in heaven"* (make Earth like Heaven...loving one another*)*.

Then there is verse eleven. *"Give us this day our daily bread"* (give us everlasting life*)*.

Now, I will go to verse twelve. *"And forgive us our debts, as we forgive our debtors"* (cancel bills...let us not hold the creditors/lenders accountable...let go of the ill feelings against hatred acts).

The last verse thirteen is a great one. It has a strong punch. *"And lead us not into temptation, but deliver us from evil: For thine is the kingdom, and the power, and the glory, for ever. A-men`"* (keep us from sin...and dare to do evil. God is the ruler and controller of everything and He deserves all the praise, always*)*.

Jesus taught us how to make it more personable when talking to God. We should start off first by saying "Our Father." We have to acknowledge that God is our Father.

Heaven and earth were made separate (but not because of human sinning). God had created Heaven and earth separately "before" we had ever sinned (God knew, but still gave us a choice to choose between right and wrong). Jesus asked for it to be loving and peaceful here on earth like it is in Heaven. Instead of next time wishing and saying for the world to come to an end (it will, one day), we should be praying to God to help us turn this baby around, so He can be pleased about what we become.

Each day we need some nourishment to help us survive. We should be nourishing off God's Words until we never get enough of reading it and want more and more. If we believe in God's Son, Jesus, who was sent by God, He can give us everlasting life. We have God's Word to keep us going. Jesus emphasized that we cannot live only on food but when we feed on God's Word we will never be thirsty or hungry again.

Creditors can be harsh in getting us to pay back and use certain tactics, such as foreclosures, repossessions, evictions, etc. Some lenders are shady by charging too much interest, conniving, doing illegal schemes, adding large penalties, and some may even do harm to your body, etc. Even all of those who are bad harsh lenders we still have to forgive them with their shabby dealing. Yes, we have to forgive each others' sins if we want God to forgive ours. We must remember that we have not always been kind ourselves. In actuality, everyone should be complying with the "Lord's Release," which is one of God's agreements to cancel out our debts after seven years (good-bye mortgages and student loans, etc.).

Some things and some people come across your mind for a reason. If a person is on your mind, just out of the blue, you need to pray for him or her. It is not a reason to start gossiping about them. Instead pray for that person then hand it over to God and then say, "in Jesus' name." You will see how fast you will stop thinking evil things about them. The Holy Ghost will keep us from giving in to that type of evil temptation. The Holy Ghost teaches us what to say at the right time. God is the Holy Spirit, which is the Spirit (the Holy Ghost) that is within us. God has always been loyal to us. He has always showed us a route plan on how to stray away from evilness. We just have to take it.

Some things that you pray about requires a little more of you. Some prayers require fasting with praying in order to be healed, to be removed, or to be accomplished. When you are down and out, you can always use God's Word to pick you up, or when you are sick to get you well. Jesus was able to rebuke the devil's demon out of a man's son that was a lunatic. The disciples were not equipped to remove the demon. *"Howbeit this kind goeth not out but by prayer and fasting" (Matthew 17:21).* Praying alone could not accomplish this particular task. It takes more. It takes abstaining from food as well.

I recalled one day after leaving a department store this guy and I started talking about God. We talked for about an hour. He spoke about his past and his present state. He mentioned that the people going in and out of the department store do not know how quickly things can change. He mentioned that I had educated him on some things more than anyone else had done in the last two years. But in reality, he was actually teaching me a thing or two. I guess you can say that we were perfecting each other. He told me that I needed to fast often. He said that when we fast more God will talk to you more. Deep down inside, I knew that I should be fasting more, and not just occasionally (with the church, something comes up, etc.).

Can you guess what happened? What? I started incorporating more fasting and praying.

I knew that I needed a closer relationship with God. Now I am fasting one day a week, and of course, this also gave me more chances to pray. During this one day fast a week, I pray, asking God to give the food that I am not eating to someone that is in need. I was dedicating it to others. I knew God could take it and physically or spiritually feed "zilliouls" or more. I was also letting God know that He comes before food, and that we can do without physical food in order to give Him the praise to honor Him. So never say what you cannot do without something or someone. It's God that we cannot do without!

Fasting can cure some things within itself. It gives your body, especially your digestive system, time to relax from all the stuff you have put in your stomach. After doing this for a few weeks, I had seen some physical changes as well as spiritual changes. It felt different from the other times. It felt like this is what I was supposed to have been doing, and was now doing with more ease. Some people may think that fasting is hard to do. What makes it hard is that we do not do it often enough. Most of the time when we do fast we try to over compensate with liquids to ensure enough nourishment is in our system in fear that we may die of starvation or something. We have to listen to our bodies because it knows how to handle less food in our system at any given time.

I see clearly why God does not want us to stop praying. For example, it keeps your mind off other things and concerns. You concentrate more on God by putting Him first above all. It helps us to not give in to our selfish desires, but think about others. One tool I used to remind me to pray often was setting my calendar alert on my cell phone at different intervals of the day for prayer. God has a mysterious and funny way of showing you things. Not long after I had contemplated doing this, I saw it being done in a similar way on television. I thought, "okay, I guess setting my calendar alert was not a bad idea." If you do not listen when God brings something on your mind, He will find a way for you to listen to Him in another way. Even while watching television. The main idea for the alert is to avoid being wrapped up in your everyday activities but to stop and give God some praise and honor.

Jesus had often times prayed to the Father (without ceasing). When we pray to the Father, we should not doubt but have faith. I thank God for us having some praying grandmas that prayed for us as well as some praying mamas. That is reason why some of us were able to make it back home safely, all in one piece after we had left for the night, or day, and probably had done some devilish things. We did not know what was helping to keep us safe. God had already listened to their prayers. Jesus highlighted that when we pray, we should not be asking Him for anything, but He will plea for us to the Father. We should ask the Father in His name. *"And in that day ye shall ask me nothing. Verily, verily, I say unto you, Whatsoever ye shall ask the Father in my name, he will give it you" (John 16:23).* We always state in our prayers "in Jesus' name" to acknowledge the power of the name of Jesus, and to ensure we have faith to receive whatever we have prayed for when we pray to the Father. When praying, the most important part is to thank God (always put God first) and appreciate all He has done, doing, and going to do, and being grateful for Jesus, who gave His life (died and rose) for us.

Chapter 8

UNDENIABLE WITNESSES

After reading the previous chapters in this book, I know that there still may be some uncertainty on what the answer to that pondering question, if Jesus is God, the Son, or Both? Before drawing a conclusion and me not wanting you to take just my word on whether Jesus is God, the Son, or Both, I want to give you something even better, and that is some undeniable witnesses. Listen to the Holy Ghost that was given to us and who resides in us to help us obey and do God's Will. The Holy Spirit also gives us understanding. Let me go ahead and present this case with all the reputable witnesses' statements and their evidence as well as one other witness (not so reputable...LOL!).

Below are the witnesses' testimonies and evidence:

1st Witness: John the Baptist
Credentials: Baptized with water; baptized Jesus
Statement: Jesus is the Son of God; baptized with the Holy Ghost
Exhibit A: John 1:34

2nd Witness: The blind man (since birth)
Credentials: Healed by Jesus Christ
Statement: Believed Jesus is Son of God (Jesus asked)
Exhibit B: John 9:35,38

3rd Witness: Saul (persecuted God's followers)
Credentials: Preached about Jesus Christ
Statement: the Son of God
Exhibit C: Act 9:20

4th Witness: Eunuch, treasurer (queen of Ethiopians)
Credentials: After reading about prophet Esaias, Philip baptized the Eunuch and explained the gospel of Jesus Christ
Statement: Jesus Christ is the Son of God
Exhibit D: Act 8:37

5th Witness: Stephen (a disciple)
Credentials: Over the disciples' day-to-day distribution
Statement: Before being killed he had looked up and saw Jesus standing on right side of God in Heaven
Exhibit E: Acts 7:55

6h Witness: Peter (apostle)
Credentials: Jesus Christ's disciple; admitted love for Jesus
Statement: Jesus Christ was Son of the living God
Exhibit F: John 6:69

The next witness is for those that still do not believe or may just want to believe in someone else. I thought hard about presenting this particular one. Then I knew sadly that some of you might believe this one quicker than you would the other ones that have already been presented.

7th Witness: Devil (satan of evil world)
Credentials: *Keeps the gate of hell; tried to entice Jesus*
Statement: *If the Son of God*
Exhibit G: *Matthew 4:3*

Now, let me continue with another witness. Please feel free to verify any witnesses' testimonies by reviewing any of the Exhibits listed. This is my last one, but definitely not the least of my witnesses that I will be presenting in this case. However, this one is the most reputable one. We believe the doctor and always say do what the doctor says to do. Let's see what we say now as our last witness is God. Let us see what God had to say. Will we believe God and say this is true what God says is true.

8th Witness: God
Credentials: *Creator of World (everyone and everything)*
Statement: *This is my beloved Son*
Exhibit H: *Matthew 3:17*

Since we have read what the previous witnesses have said and have reviewed their evidence, let's now see what Jesus had to say about all of this. We all should be waiting to hear Jesus' testimony. His credentials are that He is the Savior of the World and He died for our sins. Jesus stated, ***"I am the Son of God."*** His statement is indicated in the Bible in John 10:36. In addition, Jesus emphasized that He came to earth to represent and to do what God, His Father wanted Him to do. Jesus mentioned that He can do nothing by Himself, and He only demonstrated what He's seen His Father God do. He had asked how could He actually be God and also attest for Himself?

Jesus mentioned beforehand to the disciples that He will no longer speak in parables to them but will speak simply enough where they could understand. When Jesus had spoken to Mary Magdalene (who could have been a witness as well), He made it easy for her to understand and to communicate back to the others. Jesus had told Mary Magdalene not to put her hands on Him yet. *"Jesus saith unto her, Touch me not; for I am not yet ascended to my Father: but go to my brethren, and say unto them, **I ascend unto my Father, and your Father; and to my God, and your God** (John 20:17).* To my readers, I am wondering, can it get any clearer than this?

However, before I start to rest this case as to whether Jesus is God, Son, or both. I want to give you an opportunity to allow one more witness into evidence. I think you may want to hear his or her testimony. You have one guess to name that witness. Yes, that witness is you. What will your testimony be? Will Jesus be God, Son, or Both? If you're thinking about taking the fifth because you do not want to speak on the matter; I want to remind you not to be like Peter (rooster who crowed) and me (as the instructor) by not telling the truth about Jesus. On the other hand, if you would like to introduce your statement as evidence that includes an answer to this pondering question, you can.

Take a few minutes and proceed to examine all the previous statements and evidences pertaining to the Biblical verses. If these reputable testimonies and other witnesses have not given you the response that you were looking for to answer that pondering question; then there is something more I would like for you to consider before rendering your verdict. I was debating as to whether or not to include the testimonies before this chapter or after this chapter, so I decided to include it in the next chapter. Let me first give you a minute to take a breathier. Some may still be a little fuzzy after reading this chapter. The next chapter will also be informative and a mind-blowing experience. Please buckle up and brace yourself.

Chapter 9

SO MUCH POWER

Since you have read the previous chapters you can go ahead and make your clear-cut determination based on the facts on whether or not Jesus is God, the Son, or Both. However, if you are still lingering on making that decision then this chapter is not only for all, but especially for you. When you read it you will get some more clarification before rendering your verdict. So, let's get this chapter rolling! This chapter will also assist you with looking further into another question that no one has dared to proposition. That question is: "How did Jesus come across so much power?" Maybe I should have reworded that question as: "Why is there so much power in the name of Jesus?"

So now, you may be thinking of all the things that Jesus had done was He not imitating Himself as the King of all kings? In actuality, Jesus was declaring that He was a

Prince. He was the Prince of Peace, and being God's Son. When God had created the earth and made men, was it not written in the in the Book of Genesis that "man was made in our image and after our likeness"? Think about this for a moment. The word, "our" meant more than one being was present and that God was not there by Himself. Keep on marinating! Could this have meant that Jesus was there beside God? *"And now, O Father, glorify thou me with thine own self with the glory which I had with thee before the world was" (John 17:5).* Yes, Jesus was with the Father God in Heaven then He transformed to come down to the earth to complete God's mission. After completion, He then left the earth to go back to Heaven to be with our Father God. Yes, Jesus did come down from Heaven, but as the Son, not as God. He came to be a witness, and to tell the world all about God's business.

Jesus had emphasized that the only way we can come to the Father God is through Him, the truth and the life. God honored Jesus, His Son the Prince of life. *"Him hath God exalted with his right hand to be a Prince and a Savior, for to give repentance to Israel, and forgiveness of sins" (Acts 5:31).* Jesus suffered and died on the cross for our sins. God raised Jesus from the dead. Our Father God also gave Jesus back the authority that He once had before coming to the earth. Jesus was ordained to judge the world by God. That's why great things happen when you call on the name of Jesus. There is so much power in the name of Jesus. It is similar to a dad letting his son run his establishment. Jesus is running God's business (the world) and doing what God wants (God's Will) Him to do.

Despite all His authority, Jesus lets us know, up front, where His power comes from. Jesus told us that He cannot do anything without God and mimics what God had done. Jesus stated that there will be a Comforter for us, the Holy Ghost, being the Spirit of Truth that will be with us and in us. God has given us the Holy Spirit, which is a part of Him, to be with us at all times, to guide us. We have to repent to God and have faith in Jesus Christ. Jesus will always be with us. Jesus is in the Father. The Father is in Jesus. Likewise, Jesus is also in us as well as the Father is in us. The reason you know this is because it shows in our actions by loving one another; and that type of love comes from the heart. Although God is a Spirit, He is Almighty and can be anything He wants to be. Jesus acknowledged that no one on this earth has ever seen God at any time. If you are still wondering, and do not believe whether God sent His Son Jesus, then His Word is not in you. We are all here to be a testifier for the gospel concerning the goodness of God, and being grateful for what He has done for us.

God loves Jesus so much that He allowed Jesus to be in charge of everything. He gave Jesus the keys to the Kingdom. *"The Father loveth the Son, and hath given all things into his hand. He that believeth on the Son hath everlasting life: and he that believeth not the Son shall not see life; but the wrath of God abideth on him" (John 3:35-36).* God loved us so much that He allowed Jesus, His Son to die for our sins. If we want to do God's work, as we say we do, then all we have to do is just believe that Jesus was sent by God. It is so important for us to believe in the Son so that we can have eternal life. Jesus demonstrated His power by healing the sick, raising the dead, and removing demons. This was proof that Jesus was legit and that He was sent from God.

We definitely have to believe that there is truly only one God. Jesus had mentioned that it was time for us to know the one and only God. If we want to have eternal life, then we have to believe that Jesus was sent by the one and only true God. The Son gave honor to God, and God replicated the same. *"That all men should honour the Son, even as they honour the Father. He that honoureth not the Son honoureth not the Father which had sent him" (John 5:23).* We have to honor both the Son and the Father. If we do not honor the Son, then we are not respecting our Father God's wishes, and we do not really know God.

Jesus had asked us not to worry but to believe in Him as we believed in God. This is why trusting and falling in love with Jesus was the best thing that I have done. God had given Jesus authorization (which is much better than the American Express Black card...LOL!). God anointed Jesus with the Holy Spirit and gave Him all power over everything. We are baptized in the name of the Father, the Son, and the Holy Ghost. If Jesus stated He could do nothing without God, why do we think we can? God sent Jesus to this earth in order for us to have eternal life. Our Heavenly Father had delegated Jesus to do the judging of us. Jesus is the only Lamb (our Redeemer through His blood) that was executed and worthy enough and He has been given permission to open the Book of Life. Yes, Jesus has that much power!

Chapter 10

WINDING UP

This book was written to help bring a clearer understanding among God's sheep, and to help those who may still be wearing blindfolds to dispose of them. It gives you a good-tight grasp on whether Jesus is God, the Son, or Both. Let me not forget my bookworms that may have went straight to this last chapter and skipped reading the previous chapters; be careful because there is a lot of important information that you missed that has clarified many things. Plus, you do not want to be partially filled up, but you want to be full with all the facts.

I did not want you to have any type of distraction as you prepared your supposition. I waited until all the facts have been presented. So, I decided to put what I believed last. Here is my point blank statement on whether Jesus is God, the Son, or Both. Please read my confession below carefully.

My Confession: *I believe Jesus Christ is the Son of God. I believe the Father is God. I believe that there is only one True God with a capital "G" and that is the Father.* **"Whosoever shall confess that Jesus is the Son of God, God dwelleth in him, and he in God" (1John 4:15).** *I believe what Jesus and God have emphasized numerous times in the Bible. I do not believe what men say. You have to read the Bible for yourself so that you can get into a closer relationship with God and listen to Him. As the older generations have best stated: "You have to know God for yourself." Father God was the one that raised Jesus from the dead. Yes, that means you have to overcome the World and believe and acknowledge that Jesus Christ is the Son of God. Even if you look around, you may see that you are the only one left standing.*

While you have gotten a better understanding of the correct answer to whether Jesus is God, the Son, or Both by reading this book, do not just take my word for it. What did the Bible state? What did the other witnesses state in the Bible? Better yet, what did Jesus state in the Bible? In the Book of John at chapter 16 and verse 25, Jesus stated that He will no longer speak in parables and will speak simple enough for everyone to understand what He is saying. Jesus made it plain when He spoke to Mary, telling her to deliver a message to His disciples. He was right to the point. He was going back to the Father, which was not only His Father, but ours too. In addition, the Father was God and was not only His God, but ours too. So tell me how is Jesus, the "G-O-D" with the capital "G." He stated it clearly for all of us to understand. It was also written in the color "RED" in the Bible, which indicated that Jesus said it (case closed). Do not forget Jesus mentioned that we should not bow down to Him and that there is only One who is "good," and it was not Himself. Jesus had always remained humble.

Some of you may also be thinking how strange it is that Jesus came from Heaven and then transformed Himself into Baby Jesus. Yet, even stranger, you can believe that the devil, who was in Heaven, came down and now able to transform himself into anyone he pleased with no problem. So tell me why you can't believe Jesus, who was also God's Son couldn't have transformed into being Mary's baby.

Many times Jesus emphasized that He was doing the Will of the One who sent Him. He did not come to represent Himself, but came on His Father's behalf. Jesus asked us, when praying, to ask the Father in His name and the Father God will give it to us, not Jesus will give it to us. Even when Jesus was about to die He was still giving God His props. He stated it was not about what He wanted, but it was all about God's plan, and what God wanted. He had also mentioned that He cannot do anything by Himself, but needed His Father's help; so, how can Jesus be God? Do you think God Almighty needed someone's help to do anything or answer to anyone? He is God and He does not have to do anyone's will. We do according to His Will. When the disciples were arguing about who would sit next to Jesus, do you think Jesus should have been able to make that type of decision, if He was God? Jesus let them know right away that it was not His decision to make. Jesus had also made known that only the Father God knows the exact date and time when the end should come (not even Jesus knows).

In addition, do you think that if Jesus was God that He needed to be sent by anyone? We are talking about the Maker of the universe who has all power in His hands. Jesus mentioned on numerous occasions that He was sent by His Father. This lets us know that someone else was controlling the strings. It was not the Son. However, God did send His right hand Man for the task. He sent us His best. God knew Jesus would get the job done regardless of the devil running wild on earth, trying to get God's sheep.

Just as Adam represented us for our sins, it was Jesus (God's Son) who represented us to wipe our sins clean. He healed us by allowing forgiveness of our sins. We were all dead in sin and He gave us life. It's stunning to me to think that some of you really think God would leave Himself vulnerable to men, to come on this earth for the devil or anyone else to take advantage of Him. No way…and I hope you do not think so either. The Bible tells us that the Father is a Spirit and God is a Spirit, so, they are the same. There is no way you can catch a Spirit with your hand or try to catch it by bottling it up. You cannot capture Him. That's why God is almighty and powerful. No one can contain or apprehend Him nor even try to put Him on a post. We have to remember that He is God! He would not have relinquished any of His power as God in order to come on this earth. He is the one that set everything in motion.

God let us know that there are three who can be verified in Heaven, if all this is true. *"For there are three that bear record in heaven, the Father, the Word, and the Holy Ghost: and these three are one" (1John 5:7).* He let us know from this scripture that the God in Heaven is all the same as the Father, His Word, and the Holy Ghost. There is no distinction between them. God has also confirmed that on earth there were three witnesses who could verify that all of this is true. *"And there are three that bear witness in earth, the spirit, and the water, and the blood: and these three agree in one" (1John 5:8).* Jesus revealed that God is a Spirit. John mentioned that Jesus, God's Son, came by water and blood, not just water. God testified to it and given us eternal life through His Son. Both are in unity and are on one accord and they are in agreement about one thing, God's business, and not all about man's business. Do you want to have eternal life? If so, tell me why are some of you still struggling to believe that Jesus Christ is the Son of God. If you do not believe that Jesus is the Son of God then you are already condemned. Jesus informed us of who the True God is, and He told us that it was not Him. He kept emphasizing that we should keep God's Commandments by ensuring that we love everyone. When we make our confessions known to God, isn't it part of confessing that Jesus is Son of God? This is not any new math, and you do not have to figure it out. It is the same today as it has been in the past.

John the Baptist also emphasized that God, who sent him to baptize people with water, was the same God who sent Jesus His Son to baptize people with the Holy Ghost. *"And this is life eternal, that they might know thee the only true God, and Jesus Christ, whom thou hast sent"* *(John 17:3).* Not only that, but when John the Baptist had baptized Jesus with water he saw the spirit from Heaven lingering on top of Jesus' head. John the Baptist and Jesus had verified that there is only one True God. Life eternal is to know the True God and to know Jesus Christ whom God sent.

Why do you think some of the Pharisees and Jews were implying that Jesus was God? Was it because He forgave people's sins? If this was their only factor in the case, which may be yours too, then what should some of the disciples be called since they were also able to forgive sins? Does this make them God, of course not. God gave Jesus power to forgive sins, just like Jesus gave the disciples power to forgive sins. Just like we have the power to forgive people from their trespasses when they have transgressed us. God will also forgive us when we show forgiveness towards others.

Now, if you still do not believe that Jesus Christ is the Son of God, then you are making God out of a liar, and that God did not give His Son for us to have eternal life. In addition, if you believe that Jesus is Both, the Son and God and that the Father is only the Father, maybe that's why you can still say, in the same breath, that Jesus is on the right hand of the Father, but not on the right hand of God because Jesus is God. However, Jesus emphasized on numerous occasions that He was not more significant than the Father. This should also be another indicator that the Father is God. Can you tell me why there are many different denominations and educators trying to indicate otherwise? They are no better than the Pharisees were. Are they trying to be like the antichrist too, by denying Jesus Christ is God's Son, the Savior of the world?

So now, some of you might still be saying that "I know I am right, and I do not care what this book states." If that's the case, you may also be wondering are there two Gods (with a capital "G"). HEAVENLY, NO…NO!! I would like to go ahead right now and take a page from Paul on how, after trying relentlessly to get the Jews and Greeks to believe and understand correctly, Paul told them that their own blood was on them, and he would not be held liable. He let them know that their life was on them, he was clean, and did his job trying to tell them about God and Jesus. I will say likewise. In addition, I would like to knock the dust off my shoulder and say, "I am now clean." If you still do not understand, now it's on you. You cannot say that you were not given an opportunity to get a better understanding when the "Book of Life" is opened. Go ahead, read, and mediate on the chapters in the Bible. You may especially want to read the Book of John, Matthew, and Acts again with this new light and see if your comprehension level changes.

If we love God and one another as Jesus has requested of us, we have satisfied the Ten Commandments and have done part of God's Will. With that same love that we carry for one another, it should have us wanting to pray for one another for all things on a continuous bases. We should not want each other to fail regardless of our forte or our vocation, in which God had called us to do. We should be encouraging one another and wanting everyone to enjoy themselves and have eternal life. The bottom line is: we have to love each other and be as one as Jesus and God are one (even though separate entities). Just like husband and wife are supposed to be as one in a marriage, but separate entities. God is love and God is within us.

Jesus knew what was deep inside Peter's heart, and that was that Peter loved Him. Jesus showed Peter that even someone that loves Him could be intimidated and deny Him in times of trouble. Sometimes we can get too cocky. We have to be mindful that denying God (even unintentionally) can happen to any of us that love God. We have to be cautious and be on guard, as well as have true humility.

Yes, denying God can happen in all sorts of ways. We can deny God by keeping quiet, by our actions, by what we say, the way we treat others, etc. Since we know that there is a true God, why do we act the way that we do, talk the way we do, be silent when we should not be, etc.?

We wonder why some of God's sheep are confused, stumbling, and scattered. It is because we are giving off mixed signals. We have to stop that, and start utilizing the Bible every day. The Bible is the only Book in the world that has been tested countless of times and it has proven it's authentication. It is the most sought after Book to try to discredit. God's Word is the Truth. The Bible is the real deal. God has not changed. He is the same today as He was in the past when our ancestors believed that Jesus was the Son of God. If you need a better understanding, you need to ask God, and He will reveal it to you. To reveal understanding to you, God will lead you to the right Bible verse(s), or someone might tell you, or, He might tell you Himself. Isn't God awesome?

Remember, even if you are working in your forte while you are waiting for your calling, God is still preparing you for what He has planned for you to do. You will find that it may be totally different from what you had set out to do. Just go ahead and start listening to Him, He is calling you. When you do decide to answer your calling, just watch your life change and unfold like never before. You will see that your new walk with God will give you peace and joy.

Just as Jesus wanted His disciples to know that neither of them was better than the other one and Jesus himself was also a servant. Therefore we are also all servants. Not only did Jesus let us know that He was no more significant than God, but the only way to God was through Him. We should glorify God through glorifying Jesus.

I am hoping by now that you did not or do not base your decision on what it looks like, but make your decision on what it actually is. That is what is right and true. We should make sure we are well rounded in God. We should be reading our Bible daily and not just on the weekend. We then should make plans to read the Bible in its entirety. Then, do not stop there, but read it again and again. Just keep reading it! Each time you read the Bible, it will be better than the previous time. It is just like when you train for work. You learn all you can to learn your job and read your job manual more than once. Just as my grandma used to say, "Do not be wishy-washy"! The same is when it comes to learning all about God, which is more important. You need to learn all that you can. Do not be concerned about what other people's motives (like I was) are when being asked that lingering question whether Jesus is God, the Son, or Both. You should gladly go ahead and say without hesitation, "What did the Bible states?" The reason is because the Bible is our guideline manual for life!